JOB SPEAKS

JOB SPEAKS

Interpreted from the
Original Hebrew Book of Job

DAVID ROSENBERG

A POET'S BIBLE

HARPER & ROW, PUBLISHERS
New York, Hagerstown, San Francisco, London

ACKNOWLEDGEMENTS

A few of these chapters first appeared in *Sun, Unmuzzled Ox, American Poetry Review*, and *The Niagara Magazine*. *A Poet's Job: Eighteen Stanzas from a New Translation of the Book of Job* was printed *hors commerce* as a broadside.

FIRST EDITION

ISBN: 0-06-067008-8

Library of Congress Catalog Card Number: 76-62922

Contents

Foreword to David Rosenberg's *Job*

Translations, as everyone knows, need redoing generation by generation. The dead must breathe again through live mouths. In the last decades, American poets have translated and retranslated with passion and inspiration, stepping to tunes borrowed from old Greek and Chinese, from new Spanish and Swedish. When poets have done the work, the dead have danced to new and foreign measure. (When unpoets undo the work, the dead remain safely dead; they know their place.) We live perhaps in a time of poetic translation, of new bodily connections among races and centuries of men.

But in modern times translation of Western religious poetry has remained largely unattempted. We learn the Buddhist gaze; we largely ignore the speech of our ancient fathers. As if this galactic portion of Western experience, this vast history of spiritual intercessions, divine and human mixed in the language of poetic inspiration, were on a secular index of the mid-twentieth century; as if holy utterance were embarrassing; as if Jehovah were become Prince Albert, to be tucked away in a monument.

When new translators have rendered the poetry of the Old Testament into modern idiom, the act has been reductive or even condescending, based on the notion that our idiom is a falling away from the prose structures available to seventeenth-century scholars. Surely the idiom of the Elizabethan streets was richer than the idiom of the twentieth-century academy, and the idiom of the Jacobean Court was richer than the idiom of the current American presidency.

But when we translate into an idiom, we choose one of many idioms available to us. In our society—maybe always, maybe in all societies—there are varieties of idiom, and new translators of the Bible have opted for the blandest, the most institutional, the least traditional.

vii

David Rosenberg has been for some years a poet to watch, even to contend with, if you are in the habit of watching or contending with poets. I have followed his work for more than a decade, aware that it grew in assurance and bravery, learning its own lilt and tone and expansiveness. I followed as well his ambitious editing—a magazine called Ant's Forefoot*—first from Toronto, later from the poetic energy-center of New York's Lower East Side. David Rosenberg's strength of mind, wit, and intelligence have devoted themselves to poetry in America.*

Then he seemed to change. He didn't change, but he seemed to change. He began to translate some Psalms—published in 1976 as Blues of the Sky*—in a poetry that took on ancient spirit in the powerful idiom of modern American discoveries. He became an ancient Hebrew religious poet writing in the rhythms of the United States.*

"With Walt Whitman as a helpful guide," says David Rosenberg in his afterword, "I found my way back to the ancient Hebrew poets of The Bible."

Not only Whitman was his guide, as he acknowledges. I hear Pound, Williams, Zukofsky, Black Mountain, H. D.: all of them modernist American poets, of whom Walt Whitman, paradoxically and undeniably, is first and greatest.

So after many years a poet has translated biblical poetry into the language, into the living body, of a vital tradition. A poet uses the rich, common speech of modern America, refined and organized by poetic tradition. David Rosenberg gives himself over to Job as a man in his own time and space, but brings with him for speech the refinements and inventions that have developed in more than a century of American poems. We are allowed, then, to read or experience Job through our ears, through our mouths, through our legs marking Job's dance: through the physicality of idiom and sound that the poet and his tradition give body to.

September 20, 1976

> *Donald Hall*
> *Wilmot, N.H.*

JOB SPEAKS

Preface

The poet who composed the *Book of Job*, probably in the seventh century B.C., did not invent the story, but adapted it from legend. Almost everybody knows the legend today, whether or not they have read the biblical poem. But the real story of Job is not in the legend; it's in the telling itself, the dramatic emotion that deepens in intensity, beauty, and strangeness as the poem progresses.

The poem remains moving because the strangeness of Job's conversation with a difficult God is not alien to us. It is a persistence toward the open, foreshadowing an acceptance of the unknown, that leads us to rise in recognition of a truth beyond the individuality of our eyes, one we can't see but only feel beyond us in the power of metaphor. As we continue to understand our relatively small place in the universe, our pride in being human needs the reassurance of Job's outspoken conscience, as he faces physical and psychological demands that hold a full-length mirror to our imagination.

Most of Job's story is given in a few narrative passages beginning and ending the book; the bulk of the writing, beginning with the third chapter, becomes a dialogue between Job and a few friends, followed by God's answer from the whirlwind. The speeches of Job's friends are not as substantial as Job's, and Job's speeches reflect their arguments. His resistance to rigid dogma prevails in the end; as Maimonides wrote a thousand years ago in his *The Guide of The Perplexed*, "You will find that in the prophetic revelation that came to Job and through which his error in everything that he had imagined became clear to him, there is no going beyond the description of natural matters—namely, description of the elements or description of the meteorological phenomena or

1

description of the natures of the various species of animals, but of nothing else. For what is mentioned therein in the way of a description of the firmaments and the heavens and *Orion* and *the Pleiades* occur because of their influence upon the atmosphere.''

Job's speeches carry the essence of the whole book: feeling based in experience. They ebb and flow in intensity as the book does in its entirety. Just as the history of Israel has provided a testament to the experienced joys and despairs of community, we can experience unspeakable suffering and faith through the Joban poet's transmission of a deep, fierce love of individual conscience that is Job in his speeches.

So I have decided just to translate Job's speeches. Like many scholars have suggested, I feel they are the original heart of the book. I feel as though the original Joban poet returned to other parts of the poem at different stages of his life, that the complete *Book of Job* was his life's work as *Leaves of Grass* was Whitman's.

Job Speaks

Chapter 3

Rip up the day I was born
and the night that furnished a bed
with people to make me

the pillow from every night I lived
smother that day   cover its light
so God can forget it

let death's shadow
hold the ether mask there
clouds obliterate it

a total eclipse
blackout
swallow it a tiny pill

and that sweat that night beginning me
black oil absorb it
a hole drilled deep in calendars

shrivel that night in the hand of history
let it soften in impotence
turn off its little shouts of pleasure

every science unsex it
genetic biology   advanced psychology
nuclear bomb

no next morning shine on it
through the afterglow
singeing the eyelids of dawn

because it didn't shut the door
of the womb on me
to hide my eyes from pain

why couldn't I have been
a lucky abortion
why were there two knees

waiting for me
two breasts to suck
without them I could have stayed asleep

I could have melted away
like spilled semen
in transparent air

wrapped up in quiet dust
with gods of power and influence
and the emptiness of their palaces

with rich families their money
paper houses
for plastic children

with criminals who can't break loose
there they rest with tired workers
no more hell from bosses or jailers

who all fall down
under one blanket
not the simplest machine to serve them

why should someone have to live
locked in a miserable spotlight
bitter inside

waiting for a death far off
they search for it restlessly
like the final person in a late-night bar

they can't wait to see the iron gate unlock
and the little grave plot
comforts them

why should someone have to walk around
blinded by the daylight
he can't wave off

that God throws on him
waiting at every exit
in front of me

a table of sighs to eat
and moaning
poured out like water

every horror I imagined
walks right up to me
no privacy no solitude

and my pain
with my mind
pushes rest aside.

Chapter 6

Weigh my anguish
heave my misery on that scale
heavier than a planet

a scale filled with sand
that's how words fail me
God's arrows spinning past me

poisoning my spirit
wearing me away
little petty arguments

would you like only egg whites
no salt to season
every meal

the soul blanches
dizzy at the sight
of my own white flesh

I hope God will change this prayer
white paper hope
to violence of reality

crush me
snip off my life
paper

what a relief
I'd leap with delight
that departing train of pain

knowing I broke no law
but where to get some strength to wait
cold patience

a head of stone
skin of metal
nerves frozen dead

no help from inside
I can't reach in there
anymore

sick spirit
my dear friends
disappearing frightened nurses

and snow falls
over mouths of pure water
hidden high in mountains

of themselves
sheer ice cliffs
face my simple thirst

spring comes
they dry up
fast as a mirage

caravans lost
looking for what they thought
new roads

new places
fresh faces
tricked

by nature's technology
human nature's
idiocy

and that's how you look at me friends
panicked
into your empty words

do I say give me
things or money
save me from enemy

pay my dues for me
so talk straight I listen
at my open mistake

honesty so easy to take
but not the "advice"
unsheathed metal

to pain me with words
and deaf to mine
the wind blows away

do you lecture disaster victims
high-pressure a friend
stab love full of arguments

now look at me
face into face
no place here to glibly hide

think again—your thinking stopped
as in a blind spot
you passed my integrity

my face wide open
as I speak
my tongue there true

not as if I couldn't taste
bitter fruit
my words in my mouth.

Chapter 7

We're all somebody's workers
in a big factory
grasping for breaks

reaching for paychecks and prizes
here I'm paid these empty months
heavy nights awarded

to lie down and wait
for getting up
dragged through toss and turnings

body dressed in a texture of scars
little white worms of skin
while days run on smoothly

through a tape recorder
to run out
beyond machine of hope

mouth making a little wind
eyes straining harder
to finally disappear

in front of others' eyes
as clouds breaking up
we fall beneath the ground

we don't go home again
house doesn't know me
so nothing holds me back here

listen to this mind in pain
this "educated" soul
in words it complains

am I some Frankenstein
to be guarded
can't go to sleep alone

find some dream waiting
to terrify me
break my neck

only to find it there again
why not a hand instead
to really choke me

shake hands with despair friends
I have all day
it's all one little breath

so leave me alone God
why think up a man
think so much of one

to open it for inspection
every morning
test it every breath

look over there
somewhere other
give me just one free moment

to swallow my spit
what did I do to hurt you
man watcher

what can you be making
what cosmic thought
I'm necessary for

you hold me here
insignificant comma
like a tie in a railroad track

why not forgive
forget
I'll just settle down in dust here

you won't have to think
to even look
for me.

Chapter 9

However true
we don't know how to win a case
against God

for every question we'd ask
there are a thousand
over our heads

however high and headstrong
who among us   heart of stone
is hard enough to resist him

he picks up a mountain
it doesn't even know it
and throws it down

when he's angry
he gives the earth a little kick
and it trembles

he brews up a storm
to hide the sun
erase the stars

he laid the universe out
on the blackboard of space
alone with himself

he paced up and down
thinking something
that charmed the primitive sea

his thoughts clear as stars
laid on the surface
of a calm sea

he passes by
and we don't see him
as our heads swell with impressions

each day
sometimes bitter
we'd say "wait, wait a minute,

what are you doing?"
but he has passed us
long ago

all the gods of human history
couldn't raise a whisper
to slow him down

so what could I say
to turn him
around

even if I'm right
even if he heard
a little murmur of human truth

it would only be irritating
stopping him for even a moment
he'd knock the breath out of me

as he brushed
a fleck of soot
or tear from his eyes

(he is the means
to make justice
his end)

I could be right
and my mouth
would say something wrong

totally innocent
and my words
wrap around me

in a cloak of pride
but I'm innocent
I don't care about myself

I don't know my life
as if it makes any difference
we're all destroyed together

guilty   not guilty
some disaster strikes
mixing innocence with despair

and someone is laughing at his experiment
the whole world is wrapped
in a cloak of pride

like a prize scientist
of pride   white and clean
it's all a desperate show

the faces of our judges are covered
with the gauze
for this human play

and he made it   you
who can prove
I'm a liar

my days print out
faster than a computer
they're gone like Western Union boys

fleeing from the horror
of "progress"
exploded bombs

if I say
I'll put on a happy face
grit my teeth grin and bear it

some inner torture takes over
every time   I can hardly believe it
you'll never let me go!

my life is a sentence
why should I struggle
in these chains of words

I could wash my mouth with soap
my hands in lye
and you'd drop me into some ditch

and I'd fall on my face
until I couldn't even laugh
or challenge his force

I'd hate myself
as if all my clothes
turned into prisoner's clothes

he isn't a man
with a hand to put a summons in
was I ever in a court

can my mind come up with a court
some kind of referee or witness
to step between us

let him put down that club
that terror of naked space
he holds over me

then I could find myself
put on consciousness openly
but he won't let me be.

Chapter 10

My soul is sick of life
pushes me to speak
to fill the air with wounds

don't leave me hanging God
let me see the case
against me   is there honor

just to cut me down
to think so little of the work
that flowed from your hands

that you sit back watching the mean
arrogantly misshapened
bask in the spotlight

and can you see through the tiny eyes of men
eyes of flesh
in the little prism of a day

are your years our years
that you make me suffer in
that you enter to turn upside down

though you only you know I'm guiltless
where could I escape
beneath your hand

hands that molded me alive
and now reach in to crush me—
remember the mud you cupped for me

it's only the same dust I can return to
the dust on the bottle of milk
you poured me out of

worked me up into something solid
like rich cheese
wrapped in a beautiful skin

and inside the dream architecture of bones
you filled me with breath and vision
a vision of reality a love

but you cloud these things in a mind
of your own
a sky I know the stars stretch back from

containing all time forever
you surround me with clouds
like a lens

to see if I will
with this little mirror of a mind
think I can escape

cloud myself in nerve
and if I do—God help me
and if I'm innocent I better not look up

drunk with shame
drenched in this misery
of myself

if I stand up you come to me
cold as a camera
your pictures are marvelous pictures

they multiply your anger toward me
frame after frame
an army of moments against me

why did you pull me through the womb
locked into the brutal focus of time
I could have died inside never breathed

no one come to look at me
a quick blur in the world
carried stillborn from womb to tomb

so few days this life
why not just leave me alone
let me smile a little while

before I go off never to return
into the deep shadow of death
utter darkness—the thing itself

stripped of the background darkness
into the flaming
sun of darkness.

Chapter 12

Of course you're all so cultured
when you die (what a loss)
wisdom dies with you

but I have a mind too
working just like yours
who doesn't anyway?

yet you come by almost laughing
at a man who called out God
and was answered

and in that innocence
I'm an idiot in a showcase
for all those comfortably hidden

in the things they've accumulated
a sideshow in a pit
for you thinking you're not trapped

looking down on me as if I'd slipped
out of weakness   out of love
for an immaterial illusion

a dreamy escape
while thieves pile up things in their houses   any man
sneers behind his mask at God

secure in his heartless estate
anything his hand can grab onto
is god enough for him

look at his dog or cat
and think where they came from
the pigeons flocking in the park will tell you

look at the ground and it will tell you
with the flowers on its blanket
covering over ages of living things

fish in the sea will speak to you
as you have to me bloated with words
you mouth as if you've learned

learned to mouth without feeling
we all everything swim from God's hand
everything we make with our hands

he put in front of us
and in time ahead of us
as we begin from little fish with tails

don't our mouths know what food is
and what tastes foreign
as our ears know what words

swim to the heart
does it matter how long we've lived
do we pile up wisdom in our nets

or do we dip them again every day in the river
because wisdom flows only from God
he feeds the mind

if he breaks a living thing apart
we can't rebuild it
if he shuts the door on a man

there is nothing there to open
no rain and the earth dries up
he lets the water loose we're immersed

he's the source of energy and reflection: wisdom
the power-mad and the slave
dissolve to the same source dissolve in the mirror

and if he wishes
the wise are stripped of their wisdom
judges go mad in their courtrooms

the belt of power slips from the wearer
clothes don't fit them
like poor men in mental wards

priests are stripped and led away
money slips through the hands of the rich
like water

those most full of confidence
lose their voices
men we trust lose their senses

heirs and those next in line
have contempt poured on their heads
mantles of power shrink out of shape

the muscles of strongmen are water—
death plots spawned in the dark
are totally exposed

like negatives to light
death's shadow is immersed
in light

he swells nations to greatness
then deflates them
a nation is swept off its feet

the minds of its leaders are blown away
scattered like old newspapers
blown through a cemetery

they grope for some kind of light switch
in an ancient tomb
they flail like men overboard

drunk on their own power
they stagger toward a caved-in door
in some ancient bar.

Chapter 13

My eye has seen it
my ear heard and grasped
the vision

I know what you know
nothing less
than you

so I'd speak to God
to the one
whose reason is all

you are all plasterers
you think you are doctors
but it's only broken walls before you

you smear them over
with a whiteness of lies
a color you take for truth itself

you should shut up before them
and your silence become
a road to wisdom

stop then on your way
here on these lips
is a little plea

you speak for God
and in that acting
you can only be false

you have a case amorphous as air
the court is only a conceit
behind your forehead

what can you say
when you catch him
in a lie or contradiction

will you make him squirm
can you make him speechless
in his witness?

his words will unmask you
your conceit crack and fade
like a painted smile of piety

you will crack in the sun
of his majesty and fall
to pieces before him

your heavy talk in the dust
of ashes
with the clean little homilies

the niceties broken like clay
lay there then in your dumbness
so I may speak

opening to whatever
becomes
of me

my flesh may become
the one last meal
in my mouth

my breath become
the one last drink
in my hand

though he slay me
yet these words stand
to speak up

to his face
they are my voice itself
no false witness

could find these words
you see I'm not cut off
stand back   listen

to the voice of poetry
that is making my case
and may be lasting justice itself!

who else is there
to argue with this song
cut the air out of my life

then I'd rest content with silence
death sentence
but still two things more

I ask of you
to allow me to open
myself in your eyes

remove the hand that falls
leaden on me
like a heavy depression

except that I move   falls
like silent terror
except that I speak

and lighten my fear
I want to walk out of the dark
to meet your fierce stare

call me and I'll be there
just as right now I'm speaking
for you to answer here

how many crimes and untold lies
am I unconscious of
how can I see them

with your face hidden
veiled in silence
what enemy is in me

that you squeeze in a vise
but at such distance
infinite space

am I a leaf spun away
in a burst of wind
impossible to see

what power in that leaf
blindly afloat
to feel terror

this numb piece of paper
you squeeze my feelings on
held in this painful air:

bitter words
you have written down
against me

a list I inherit
from the unspoken lies
of my past

my feet are also locked
as if you would hold me
ready for punishment

in that vise
some crime some slight
some monstrous pinprick

forced you to look
narrowly at me
narrowing my path

noting each unique footprint
brand of a slave
a voice singing out through the bars.

Chapter 14

Man swims out of a woman
for a few days of restless living
full of anxieties

a flower springing up
under the passing cut
of the share's thrust

a shadow fading out
of time
gone

disintegrating
like an old wineskin
an old coat

eaten away
by moths
drained

and this is the creature
you open your eyes on
take time to judge

as if pure earth can be extracted
out of lust-spattered hair
by a man himself

however young or innocent
he dies
in a dusty coat of experience

because our days are numbered
so we can count them ourselves!
approximate the whole

short story
you give us
with its "The End"

look the other way   turn your eyes away
why don't you
just let us be here

ignorant slaves
enjoying our work
enjoying our sleep

till we finish this simple story
and get a little rest . . .
even a tree cut down

has some hope
it can spring to life
old roots

start up tenderly
even if its body stump
dies in the dust

soon as it whiffs some water
it starts
growing like a new plant

but a man just disappears
one last breath
and where is he

lakes have completely evaporated
rivers shrunk away
and men laid down to rest

never to rise
or materialize
the sun can die

galaxy collapse
space evaporate
universe shrink to a ball

and we will not hear it
nothing will shake us
awake in our beds

if only you could hide me
beyond existence
outside of space and time

in a darkness
a secret
beyond the known

until your famous anger passes
and then you remember me
waiting for the book to close

waiting for an appointment!
is it just possible
a man dies and lives again?

I'd bear any day   every day
heavy as it is
waiting

for your call
and I would answer
you want to hear me again

this creature you made with care
to speak
to you

but now you number each step I take
note so slight a false movement
I can't even see it

as if my guilt is sealed
under a coat of whitewash
faded from my eyes but there

as a mountain
that will finally fall
a rock that will be moved

a rain wearing away the stone
a storm a flood
washing the earth away

as you wash away
the hopes of a man
we are lost at sea

our faces go blank
unrecognizable
painted out forever

sunk out of your sight
we swam a little
and we drowned

our families rise in the world
we don't know them
or they fall

or they disgrace themselves
sink into despair
we don't think of them

we only feel our own flesh
rotting   only hear
the echo of our body:

the pains of its dying,
the mourning
of its self.

Chapter 16

I've heard these righteous clichés
over and over
thanks for the precious comfort

the heavy breathing
in a bag of wind
that just gets noisier

you want to drown me out
with monotonous whispering
platitudes?

I could do that if I were you
like putting any word in front of the next
while making faces at a baby

the tone is one of a sermon
you solemnly deliver
with just the right voice quiver

babble on
till the baby falls asleep
but when I really speak

my pain stays there
and if I hold myself back
I'm still alone with it

and him
his famous jealousy
wearing me down

like precious jewelry
over my entire body like skin
each minute becomes heavier

I'm distracted by myself
alienating all my company
who turn on me

like bribed witnesses—
the friends I counted on!—
lying into my face

friends who've disappeared
like flesh on my body
thinned by tension

wrinkled by despair
slim enough to be accused
as I'm barely standing

of paranoia or hunger
therefore craving bread
therefore a liar to myself

whose open face
hides these hot words
steaming in my mouth

but it's clear I'm consumed
on the flame of his anger
in the gnashing of teeth

in the eyes that flash
sirens across my face
the mouth that curls in a snarl

an arm reaches out a claw
slaps my face
my friends become a mob a beast

with the faceless energy called courage
of a bitten animal
raw violence

selfish masks
ripped away from the unconscious
faceless the way they really are

and I'm delivered
by my God
to this transparent world

of bitter losses vicious plots
covered with a veneer
of paper thin consciousness

the masks of sincerity
dropped like hot coals
in God's rage against me

I was content
happy productive peace-loving
peace-making

until he grabbed me by the neck
spun me around
and shattered me

worried me to pieces
pulled me together a moment
to stand as a target

for friends and enemies
what's the difference
I could be them

blindly righteous
strangers to ourselves
we think our eyes are friends

confidently looking out for us
but they'd close in the instant
they saw the volcano within

the first volcano
and when we turn to look back at the world again
it's almost too dim to see

slowly we adjust to the light in the room
this is the world we're made for
but where is the human light

of justice coming from—through the crack
within   or from without
but space is all the same

and on both sides I'm a target
God's arrows spinning past me
his men surround me

and I'm hit
again and again
piercing my stomach my bowels

spilling my insides out
he clubs me down
leader of the riot

or the purge the pogrom
he is a policeman
and I am wearing rags

can't change my clothes
can't shave can't move
my life my plans paralyzed

till my head sinks into dust
heavy antlers
of a battered wild ram

humiliation
my face a red desert
from weeping

craters of depression
the dark eye shadow
of death

and not a drop or speck
of violence
from my own hands

not a bad wish
not a curse in the cleanness
of my daily creations

O earth, cover not over my blood!
don't be a tomb a museum
for my miserable poem

my cry against this sinking
leave my voice uncovered
a little scar on your face

face of the earth
open to the sky
the universe

where you can see
a justice waiting to be discovered
like an inner referee

the deep seat of conscience
where a creator sits
handing me these words themselves

these verses are my absolving witness
on this little home earth
from which they speed

out into the universe forever!
even as my tears
fall in the dust

before an angry God who hears and sees
my plea   words and tears
of a man

for the life of his brother or son
the love of another living man
who is also me

on the outside
and inside the listening unconscious
creator who is also he

as clear as the clearest dream
as the little ball of earth
seen in a photograph

whom I call with my breath
as if he were human
unlike these words living beyond me

for I know I'm sentenced to die
my little story of years
will soon be over

I'll be going down the road
to fall in the dust
just one time.

Chapter 17

My breath straining
my days fading
through a prism of pain

in my chest
thinning my voice my hair
getting me in shape

for the grave
surrounded by a chorus
of mockingbirds

who won't let me rest
my eyes wide open
on the hard bed

of their bitterness . . .
lay down something beside me
some collateral I can grasp

you yourself
granted me this speaking
no one else will back me

no one shakes this open hand
you've closed their minds
shrunk their hearts into a bird's breast

but you won't let them sing
over me   in the morning
because they're shut in their ignorant night

denying a friend
for some self-righteous flattery
precious blinders for their eyes

while their children's sight grows dim
who recognize my famous name
trademark for bad medicine

something to spit at the feet of
my eyes are also blurred
but by tears

my hands and feet
fading away
like shadows

if any man is really open
he'll stop in his tracks
at this trial

of standing up
on innocent feet
among brothers

and being covered with total abuse
still that man will walk on
through the heap of civilized refuse

the wasteland of clichés
spiritual materialism
and his legs will grow stronger

meanwhile the show goes on
men of the world
stone me

with the ready-made knowledge
any idiot can buy in the supermarket
my business totally collapsing

my days fading like an echo
of the shattering
of my ego   all my plans

my heartstrings
cut silently
in the night that switches to day

at the push of a button
like the unconscious habit
of false righteousness

taking the powers that be
for granted
and so I can't even sleep

you come to me with these rigid proverbs
these artificial lights
like "there's light at the end of the tunnel"

all I want to see is reality
of darkness   to make my bed
underground

grave you are my father!
worm my mother
and my sisters

so here I am in the dust
faithfully returned to
so this is the hope

I should bow down to?
where are we then
but in the fading light of the unconscious

turning dreams to lost memories
dreams of a decent life
who can see anyone else's   *but him*

the innocence of them
spontaneous trust
my spirit open to them

will they also go down with me and with
these dream mouths of friends
to the ancient bar of dust

the vast unconscious cellar
to become dry bones
all my dreams of a livable future.

Chapter 19

How long does this gale
of words go on
this wind

you turn on my spirit
choking me
each time you've opened your mouths

is an insult friends
a hot brand on me
cast-iron reproductions of advice

meant for sheep
it doesn't offend you
to goad me like one

let's say I did something wrong
it's none of your business
no example for your self-righteous

spiritual merchandise
the goods making you feel superior
as if this rag of skin is proof

of my poverty
open your ears your silk purses
a minute: it's God who's

done me wrong
this chain around my neck
is not my words or thoughts

if I cry help
I'm being strangled
no one can hear

where's the judge
to hear these groans
from a poor man

I'm locked in my own ghetto
the streets are dimmed
by walls of pain

my pride stripped away
my humble crown of faith
in my own work and spirit

knocked down
my body a truth horribly distorted
I'm nothing

torn down like an old building
gone before you know it
a vacant lot

paved over
not even the hope of a tree
my smallest hope makes him angry

kindling for his rage
I'm the enemy
surrounded by his troops

with your ironclad masterplan
cut off the city
as if I were some Leningrad

but my brothers are far away
removed   remote
my friends totally aloof

relatives don't know me
my closest friends
don't remember who I am

guests in my house
never knew me
to neighbors I'm the worst kind of stranger

an immigrant a beggar a bum
in the eyes of women I supported
invisible to men who worked for me

even when I ask them humbly
as a poor dog
a few tender yelps

an intimate embrace a kiss
fills my wife with horror
just the smell of my breath

my whole family is disgusted
backing off
coughing in disgust

children on the street
hold their noses   spit
run from me

all my deepest friends turn away
can't stand the sight of me
all those I loved the best

my bones creak laughing at me
my skin loose around them
like toothless gums   leprous

my teeth disappearing
there's hardly one left or anything solid
holding me together

some pity friends a little pity
dear friends
I'm wounded   struck

by the hand of God
a serious blow you can see
why do you keep on hurting me

why is the pleasure of my flesh not enough
that you need to squeeze
the last breath from my spirit

O if only these words were written down
printed and reproduced
in a book

engraved carved
with an iron pen
into solid rock forever!

monumental inscription
filled with volcanic lead
hardened into my one solid witness!

but inside myself
I know my witness breathes
to answer me   God himself

giving birth to words
vision itself
my constant creator

an answering wind like out of my mouth
to turn my case around
in front of the world

my judge and referee
and I'll be there
even without my flesh

though cancer devours my skin
I'll stand up   behind this body
my spirit will somehow pull me up

even for a moment to see it
in the twinkling of an eye
through the open window

of my own eyes
still alive
my living heart feeling

the justice of his presence
beside me within me
before I die

as I almost did
when you joined the bandwagon
of my pain

waving at me to stop
as if it was all my fault
as if I started the engine

but you'll stop at a whistle friends
that blows you down
that blows your spiritual arrogance away

the sound of your own pain
opening your eyes
to a higher judgment.

Chapter 21

Just listen to me
you're all sealed up
in the big consolation

of blind faith
that you offer me so generously
but if you'd just open a little hole

in your ears
I'd be happy enough being alive
speaking these words to living beings

then you can resume mocking
anyway it's not you not men
pushed me to voice my thinking

to have to speak my mind
total consciousness
to listen to my own self calling

to hear all and nothing
the answer in the call
more than one man can stand

so what good is patience
look at me head-on
and be amazed

as your hand jumps
to cover your mouth
gaping astonished

when I stop to think
myself
I'm paralyzed

my skin crawls
pure horror
here it is   hear it

why do totally corrupted men
go on living
grow old in style

grow richer every day
see their children grow
into their power and houses

in safety   insured
peace to them
and their brothers

God's arrows
don't reach them
no heavy justice for them

their bulls mount their cows
no sooner said than done
a calf without fail

they have a flock of children
frisky little lambs
they run out to play

and dance to the tambourine
and sing with the lyre
and absorb the melody of flutes

their lives close like a sunset
prosperous and peaceful
they head to the grave

go down softly under
and yet
they'd said to God

leave us alone
we don't want to know
of you

why do we need God
to be servants
and what's there to get

from meditating on it
what's the profit
in spending our time on him?

isn't their happiness
in their own hands
isn't this circle of corruption

outside God's orbit
as you think of the unscrupulous
do you see their lights

turned off
their careers in ruins
bodies struck by heavy hand

because God is mad at them?
how often
and do you see them turned

to rags
yesterday's newspaper
blowing in the wind

you say his children
will end up paying for it?
no—let his own nerves

strain for the price
his own eyes
see himself break down

a shattered mirror
blown apart
in a heavy wind

let him live and learn
and drink from the cup
that's thrown in his face

what does he know or care
how his house stands
like a man totally drunk

he's finished the bottle
of his life
died satisfied

is there something God should learn
from us
here

something about spiritual materialism
the debt he owes and forgot
to pay the corrupt and yes the self-righteous

because you yourselves
become his judge
when you write off the reality

of the world he made
set in front of you
just as it is

one man dies at a healthy age
drinking to the full
his milk pails were always full

marrow of his bones still sweet
body still attractive
to women   attracted by them

and another man dies shrunken
in a bitter spirit
not even a drop of happiness

and then they lie down together
in the same bed of dust
with worms to cover them up

and yes I know your thoughts
the wooden arguments
the corpses you're lining up

you want to ask your rigid questions
but where *is* Stalin's house now
or Franco's

not to mention countless
run of the mill criminals
never caught: Martin Bormann etc.

the loyal collaborators
the rich and privileged saluting
any flag that flies their way

reflected in the polished boots of chauffeurs
Mercedes Benz
certain popes

and busy in the wings the faceless
you won't see them standing around
at any apocalypse

you ought to ask some tourists
who speak your language
open-mindedly

listen to some impartial camera clicks
look at the photographs
even postage stamps

you push me into irony
and out the other side
to common sense

the deeply corrupt disappear
in limousines and passports
flown to obscure small towns

or islands
relax or even return
after the dust settles

and newspapers have crumbled
no one stings him with pointed proverbs
under his beard

no one unmasks him face to face
he lives like a god
and dies on the shoulders

of the mass of dupes
who carry him to his grave
which becomes a protected museum

his mouth is fixed at peace
by the embalmer   the priest
throws no dirt on his reputation

he'll live in some history
while the masses supporting him
are barely a footnote

Hollywood extras
following the hearse
lining the curbs

why this empty comfort you point to
these empty nothings you argue
this empty room of thought

you goad and push me into
this dark and hostile consolation
this humorless nonsense of empty religion.

Chapter 23

Today again
my speech my poem
this hard-talking blues

this heavy hand
from the long deep writing
of my spirit

O if I could know
where to go
and there

find him
at home
in his seat of justice

I'd sit down there
to lay out my case
before him

my mouth would be full
like a river
of what my heart must say

my mind open
like a window
to hear his words

as easy to understand
as the sounds of people
on the street

I wouldn't be blown away
overpowered
by them

but my own voice would be steadied
like a tree outside
in a bracing March wind

wind between the wood
earthly music
stirring my spirit

in his house
where an upright open man
isn't afraid to confront him

to listen to respond
to contend   a human music
creating the air

for a higher justice
in which to hear
I'm set free

but now I look to the east
and he isn't there
west and a vast empty ocean

face north
like a true compass
see nothing

turn south
and he's still invisible
hidden from my ear

but he follows each step I take
even when I'm sitting doing nothing
and he puts me in the crucible

to have his gold
because I've walked all my life
toward his light

past the neon temptation
of unreal cities
surreal commercials for "normality"

my lips have opened
for his infinite word
in meditation

I've opened his book
in my heart
and read with open eyes

he is one
determined within himself
as end

and has an end
all changes all choices
rest in his mind

but how can I change his mind
his soul desires
and it's already been done

ancient history
past changing
beyond our time

here he hands me
part of a sentence
already out of his mouth

and there's more to say
just as the past fills
with more to discover

it makes me shiver
to think
I must face him

here on this earth
now in this life
present in the infinite

transfigured
as my inaccessible inner self
rises to his hand

I turn white
cold sweat of fear
washes across my face

I want to turn back
as if I'm walking in my sleep
out of a world I know

my own shadow
smiles back at me
a shadow in the night

the past is drunk with strangeness
and his presence
drowns my heart in naked space

because he brought me out here
into the darkness
where I must continue speaking

into the open
like a child holding tight
to the side of his trembling crib.

Chapter 24

The days of judgment
and everyone has one
are no dark secret

because God has finished his sentence
but men are mostly blind
and that's the way God made it

but why are his hearers
also deaf
to the coming of those days

while corrupted men
totally in the dark
cut through fences and honest agreements

and anyone in their way
knocking down the shepherd
stealing the sheep

they drive off
in the repossessed cars
of the poor

foreclose
on widows and orphans
lock up a workman's tools

shove the homeless
out of their way
terrorize old people

already cringing
in little groups
huddled in corners

and the masses
are exploited asses
donkeys up a mountain

or camels in the desert
they report for work
as they're told

as the sun rises until dark
carrying the water they can't take home
to their thirsty children

they harvest healthy food
for corrupt masters
pick the ripe grapes

for the cynical toasts
of the power-hungry
spilling the precious wine of their sweat

to finally lie down
naked under cold stars
not a shirt on their back

to wear in the predawn
dew from the mountains
making them roll over in their sleep

and hug close
a rock
shelter from the storm

when it rains
while the privileged few
snore in their yachts

on the sea of the masses
on the sweat of their backs
on the milk of a mother's breast

from whose arms they'd wring
the brief soft luxury
that's all most men ever know

rip the child
from the widow's breast
as security

against some calculated debt
to keep the heads of the poor
under water

in a sea of desperation
naked of human rights
a mass of mesmerized slaves

walking through the rich waves
of grain
bringing in the sheaves

for a perversely ornate table
half-starved
the workers of the world

between stones
pressing oil for the ruling classes
only their sweat belongs to them

treading the winepress of the bosses
in life's oasis
dying of thirst in the desert

listen to those distant groans
far from the drowning hum
of the city

a wounded army of souls
gasping in their ancient tracks
but God doesn't hear that prayer

and in the cities
even among the elite
men get away with murder

darkness meets darkness
a blood pact
against his light

light of day
of reality
of the inspiration for making

electric light
and the continuing surprise
of every morning sunrise

there are men
who've lost the path
to daylight

rising at daybreak
to terrorize the caravans
of the huddled masses

murderers
and at night under their dark blanket
thieves

adultery: another broken commandment
under cover of darkness
and masks

any form of disguise
a man in woman's clothes
slipping into the harem

thinking under his veil
no one will see me
no one know but she

they break up houses
as criminals
break into them

into the ones at night
they marked that day
in an ignorant scrawl of a mind

blind
to the light
we are given

strangers in the morning
to their own shadow
floating on the surface of consciousness

they are submerged
in the nightmare unconscious
because they can't make anything

of the light of a star
focused like a conscience
in the eye of imagination

creating light
in the image of light
honest day light

I rise from a dream in
to discover the universe without
that was within

rising past superstition
idols and dumb images
having nothing to say in daylight

yes belief requires dreams
and every night
we go to sleep in this world

while those others are at home
talking and listening
to shadows

completely intimate
with the nightmare
of death's shadow

show me
this isn't true
reduce these words to nothing

to nonsense like a magician
and I'll show you as your new servant
my eyes were fixed on reality.

Chapters 26—27

Since I'm so weak
and this poem so pitiful
so powerless

I'm lucky again today
to have such friends
such care for the feeble

how nobly you've lifted
this poor arm that writes
what a miracle

what strong donations
you've made to little minds
barely subsisting on the minimum wisdom

I can hardly know what I'm saying
except thanks to you
your fatherly advice spilling over me

but who filled you with it
and who are you speaking to
what possesses you

to form such a rigid piety
with a breath
caught in what flow of meaning

my poem has a way
to continue
even as I swear by God

who holds back my living right
to be free of bitterness
that damn it I'm speaking

my own mind as he allows
as these breaths come out of me
these shreds of phrases

my spirit revives and hangs on
to the wind God sends
through my nostrils

and the words that leap off my lips
fall true to the page
of my conscience

it's out of my hands
to let you get away
with your self-righteous platitudes

as solid as flotsam
but as long as I'm alive
I won't let go

of the stone rightness
my spiritual individuality
until I die

the page of my heart
opens to the wind
of his warming breath

let my enemy be as cold
as the heartless
my accuser suffer

the secret death chills
of the liar
perspire with the guilty

cold sweat flow
in his veins
dripping from a heart as stiff

as an icicle   a conscience
upright but hopeless
as he prays

for what help
meditates on what
burning sphere of thought

that may give him a push
through the world of things to accumulate
but what is there to get

when his body loses its grasp
on life   does God hear
the cry of this hypocrite

will he delight in his calling
man to God   a dialogue
or has this man's words been smothered

behind a mask
yes I know something about it
God's place

inside us
moving my hand
that lifts and calls

to him
it has nothing to conceal
my mind is an open book

for God's hand
take a look
you must have read there

so why have you become so proud
you blow your hot empty breath
your stream of words on me.

Chapter 29

Who can turn me around
until I find myself
back in the old days

the good days
God watching over me
the sun shining

inside me
like inner light
to usher me past the nightmares

on the screen of giddy youth
my life was in focus
around me   it was autumn

wife and children growing
my walks were bathed in light
in cream

the heaviest rocks in my way
smoothed out
like oil

I was as if transported
wherever I went
on a stream of affection

when I went out the city gates
or when I came to my place
in the city square

the younger men quickly stepped
aside   like a wave disappearing
while the older men rose to their feet

celebrities stopped
in the middle of what they were saying
and almost covered their mouths

the voices of politicians trailed off
like old newspapers
blown in the wind

their tongues dried up
dusty leaves
swept to the back of their mouths

I mean men listened to me
you could hear a leaf drop
they wanted my opinion

when I finished I was allowed
the clarity of silence
my words fell gently on them

like spring rain
they were attentive as trees
opening their arms

stretching their hands out gladly
as if their minds were open
to the sky

and when I laughed or
made light of things
they were almost stunned

to be reminded I was human
their eyes would light up
blossoms the sun smiled on

I directed their thoughts
to the best way   a revelation
they followed like actors visibly

in the presence of a master
a man who'd paid more than his dues
inspiring confidence in the disillusioned

their ears would open
and mouths speak of me
graciously

anyone seeing me
became a witness
to my openness

I embraced a poor man
and an orphan
and a man with no one in the world

to turn to
a man dying gave me a blessing
a widow smiled with joy for me

I opened myself
and a cloak of pride
slid from my shoulders

I embraced a sense of justice
that wrapped itself around me
like a warm coat in winter

I was eyes to the blind
and feet
to the lame

a father to the homeless
a light in the midnight window
to the stranger far from home

I was a destroyer of nightmares
like a gentle counselor
in an orphanage

then I said to myself
I will die
in the open arms of a family

and my seed in that nest
outgrow the arithmetic of a lifetime
the calculations of a mind

or historical lineage
my spirit extends beyond time
like a phoenix rising

from ashes
an ancient poem
from the dust of pages

my roots reaching out
for water
each new coming spring

and the dew shall lie all night
on my branches
and I feel the sweetness of that weight

on me
that miraculous touch
of heaven

waking my heart
made light again
by the fire of love within

my pen returning to the page
like an arrow to the heart
a love as strong as death.

Chapter 30

But now it's all a joke
to the younger generation
I'm an outdated ape

too heavy to take seriously
for the puppies of men
who in my time I wouldn't

have insulted my dogs by going near!
dogs whose hearts were higher
among my flocks of sheep

men whose hearts burned out
in a destruction of spirit
shriveling their humanity into rags

they haunt the back alleys
of a civilized wasteland
like the "disgusting" gypsies

they stooped to revile
in false images
to make themselves feel superior

devastated Indians
of their own manufactured
nightmares

eating the weeds
they claw up greedily
like outcast witches

banished from the self-righteous society
that rightly hounds them
like fleeing common criminals

they huddle in unblanketed pits
in primitive dreams: caves
of obsolete railroad cars

wallowing in the mud
of self-pity
gnawing the worms of desire

their sons a gang of animals
monsters of inhuman pride
hands on their belts like horsewhips

and now I've become the bait of their humor
their theme song
their saddle their fetish

their figure of contempt
they are primitive giants of ice
aloof over me

I'm the floor
they spit on
because God has knocked me down

unstrung the bow of my back
unleashed the curs
of their tongues on me

these vile witnesses at my right hand
this vigilante lynch mob
has come down my road of ruin

there are no living heroes
to step out of nowhere
in their way

all my defenses broken down
inevitably as water
breaks through an abandoned dam

my nerves on edge
wild deer fleeing
from the cracks of a thunderstorm

terror faces me like a wall
or a wind blowing my strength away
my hope disappearing like a cloud

my soul emptied like a glass of water
and in my hand
are miserable tears

my very bones are sweating
at night my veins
restlessly throb

my clothes and skin
bleached beyond recognition
by the acid of my suffering

my collar shrinks tight
around my throat
the hand of God's wrath

which drags me down to the mud
my spirit itself is dressed
in dust and ashes

I speak to you
hard and true
over the heads of men

who look down at me
my voice goes out of me
a wounded bird

flying to you
in your sky   crying
its whole being is calling

to you and you
don't answer
I stand trembling before you

and you look at me
as if I'm not there
as if you don't know or care

what I want
you sit in your great high chair
and in your great satisfaction

toy with me cruelly
your hand bears down on me
heavy and hostile

I'm like crumpled paper
lifted in your wind
driven to the edge of existence

tossed in a tempest
my significance dissolved
in the heavy downpour

without the warmth of your care
even the word significance
bleeds dry

I know your arm is leading me
to my death
to the meeting house

where every living creature
lies down
before you

but did I ever lift
my arm
to strike or sweep away

a ruined heap of a man
whose tortured voice reached out
for help   to me

for a shred of sympathy
and could I not help but weep
with him

in his hour of despair
did my heart not stop
for this man

for the poor and wretched
of humanity
didn't I close my eyes

like a hurt child to feel
the boundless passion of inwardness
in every man opened by suffering

but when I opened my eyes
looking for something hopeful
desolation

I waited for some light
I hoped for light
but darkness came over me

and in the pit of my stomach
a cauldron boils
endlessly

days flow into days
like a miserable diarrhea
I wake in the morning

and there's no sun
no ray of friendship
I stand up crying

in the squares
in the bars
in the cafés

and I'm looked at as a brother
to dragons or lizards
crocodiles are my companions

owls and screeching ostriches
are the comrades of my
plaintive shriek of despair

my skin hangs on me
like a tanned wolfhide
my bones melt with fever

my lyre is stretched
to the pitch of wailing
my flute

is a voice turned
to a siren song
in a human holocaust.

Chapter 31

I came to a decision
behind my eyes
not to let them wander

over the innocent bodies
of young girls
I refocused their attention

what decision am I thus allowed
to see reaching into this world
from behind God's highest cloud

what sense of human
natural rightness
beyond the senses

is it really disaster
for the cold-hearted
hard-core manipulators

of sympathy and affection
devastating twisters
of all feeling in their paths

doesn't he see me
standing openly in the aisle
isn't that his light each step I take follows

if I walked beside high vanity
self-made lights of deception
and let my foot pull me dumbly

into the shadows of bitterness
then let my heart be weighed like stone
on an honest scale

in his hand of justice
and he'll know the lightness
my heart still clings to

if I let my legs
carry me away
in blind animal pride

or let my heart go
to the blood-lust of the world
before my naked eyes

or let my hands indulge themselves
in the mud and gravel of cement
for a wall between us

then let another mouth
eat all
I've worked and sweated for

and all the seeds I've planted
in the ground in my mind in the body
of my wife

be uprooted   totally
if I gave my heart away
blindly

to the cold deception
of a heartless woman
or the wife

left innocently alone
in the sanctuary
of my neighbor's home

if I consciously even dreamed
myself there
let my wife swallow every drop

of my lifeblood my honor
in the seed
of every passing man

let them worship between her thighs
as greedily as men suddenly released
from death sentences

then let her rise
to become their servant
to wash their sheets while I weep for her

while my eyes go blank with despair
before the total explosion
of a life

I'd be guilty of a fire
swallowing up the air around me
destroying the spirit of others

as it's magnified in the mirror
of my silent rage within
gone blind with desperation

all my hopes dreams desires
utterly consumed
in the passionate proof

of my lifelong ignorance
boiling up within   temptation
for an untouchable woman

and forgetting that I'm a man
descended from men and women
who held their love humbly

as the free gift
of a baby in their arms
deserving adoration

if I coldly turned away
from the open heart or hand
of my humble servant

anyone I put
consciously or not
in a place to serve me

and who did so   freely or not
then where am I
when I'm in God's presence

how will I come to ask for
what no one can demand
the free gift of love

no longer mine to give
as I turned cold and heartless
in this body he gave me

that he made for us all equally
in the wombs of women
he alone   shaping us there

one creator
one hand moving
one conscious subject

if I refused
the needs of the poor
given to my spirit to bear

if I refused a woman   homeless
having lost her husband
and turned to me

a man in her eyes
growing dim with tears
someone other to look on

for help in the overpowering
needs one life faces
alone for the sake of others

if I swallowed my morsel of food
alone in the face of even one orphan
who had none

if I didn't raise that boy
as his father   that girl
as her true compass

if I've seen someone naked
hopelessly exposed
having lost the shirt off his back

or a poor man woman or saint
who barely ever had one
if that body was not a blessing

I was given to warmly embrace
with fleece from my flocks
if I lorded it

over anyone
because I had the cold advantage
of friends in high places

then let my arm be wrenched
out from its socket
my writing hand fall limp

the pen slip from my fingers
words dry up on my lips
because the turning of God

away from us   as we may turn away
is utter devastation
the dark side of the moon

I couldn't stand there
or breathe
unless he gave me some wisdom

to learn to shield myself
learning by facing terror
that love protects us

if I put my faith in gold
filled my sack of pride
with money

and talked to myself
as if I were precious metal
saying I hold my own security

if I stood up straight
held my head high
encased in rigid armor

the tin shield of fortune
I thought was self-made
forged with my own hand

if I stared into the sun   inwardly
mesmerized or blindly enlightened
struck by its shining riches

if I ever stood hypnotized
before the dreamlike beckoning
of the full moon rising   silver and gold

letting my heart be captured
by cults of sensuality
becoming a slave

to my own enlightenment
handed over to the power
of some physical light or master

some magical dazzling myth
obscuring the light of history on
the pages of human struggling

from generation to generation
to be free of idols and false images
and the hand holding the ax

at whose edge we tremble
dazzled by the glinting beauty
of secret fear or evil

as it slices through our thought
until we can't hold together
can't contain the reality

of opposing forces of energy
the physical struggle inside
of good and evil

if I fell
before idols
separating thought from feeling

if I kissed my own hand
to blow kisses
to some material body in the sky

then that is the height of superstition
the queen of lies
in the face of God

like incest
denying my nature
cutting off my human hand

if I secretly exulted
to learn my enemy
was cut down

struck down by his mean thought
like lightning
where he was hiding

if I let bitterness
slither through my lips
to poison his character

then let the men closest to me
pin me down
devour my flesh with passion

twisting my desire
to share with anyone hungry
my portion of meat

if I left a passing stranger
to sleep in the street
naked to darkness

and didn't open my door
to the open road
sharing my light and warmth

if I have hidden my sins
in a hole
in my heart

like the common herd
covering up the truth
with dirt and litter

because I was afraid to stand out
from the herd   afraid
of common gossip

and contemptuous eyes
of the self-righteous   boring in
with the cold severity of rock-drills

if I stood terrified at that thought
mute
crippled in the heart

afraid to open it or my mouth
to face my own weakness
the petty lies to myself

that I could not even walk
out my door
with my head on frontwards

then I would not deserve the paper
I'm writing on
but here it is!

this is my voice
reaching out for the ear
open to hear it

where is the hearing   the time and place
to make my suffering real
an indictment a list of crimes

even if it were longer than a book
I'd carry it on my shoulders
with honor

I'd wrap it around me like a royal robe
bind it around my head
like a royal turban

I'd walk up to my judge
and lay out my heart like a map
before him

this incredible gift of a heart
feeling
my true thoughts

holding the history book of my life
open to his light
light is my defense!

as confident as a prince
I'd put my life on the line
in the words that are given me

in this court invisible to me
transparent as clean air
before the judge I live to hear

and if my land cried out against me
indicting me with the tears
that ran down in furrows

man made
on the face
of the earth

if I plucked the riches
its fruit   filling my mouth
and gave back nothing

not even a thought
expanding
in gratitude

if I have planted
any cause for anger
in the minds of its tillers

if one migrant worker cried out
because I forced the breath
of integrity out of him

then instead of wheat
let my hand reap
thorns

let it force to no end
this thistle
of a pen

let weeds grow
and cover this page
instead of words that grow wheat

and here for now is ended
the poem
Job speaks.

On Translating Job

*J*ob is one of the greatest poems we have because it combines the highest passion with a constant refusal to leave the realm of experience. Job is any man because he speaks, even at the limit of human endurance, from his own personal circumstances in a speaking voice. And I face my own suppressed response to the completely other, to a confrontation of God and man, through the Joban poet's eyes. This happens in the illumination of the metaphorical power of speech. Light comes from dramatic tension the poem builds between a metaphorical creation and the creator's awareness of a higher Creator and a deeper order.

Job's confidence in his creator's existence is equaled by his confidence in himself. He discovers in the penetrating vision of his own words the same revelation that Israel had earlier beheld: in the beginning was the Word—a *human* vision of creation, resisting the mythological fantasy-images of the unconscious mind. He knows that his words have power, that he himself is an audience for them as he hears how the spirit behind them rises above his physical circumstances. The voice of the prophetic poet extends beyond the normal bounds of tasteful poetry precisely because the voice, inspiration itself, becomes larger than his own. Words themselves convey the revelation. We hear the universality of totally selfless speech.

With Walt Whitman as a helpful guide, I found my way back to the ancient Hebrew poets of the Bible. Like the Joban poet, Whitman is a conscious step past the *literal* prophets of Ancient Israel—a poet *first*. "As he sees the farthest he has the most faith,/his thoughts are the hymns of the praise of things"—that is Whitman, in "By Blue Ontario's Shore," on the necessity of spirit in the poet. In that poem as in others,

Whitman renews the Old Testament Prophets' faith in the individual. Self-examination in poetry has increased since Whitman's "Song of Myself" and corresponds to a re-discovery of ancient roots. The historical source of poetry, of the poet's visionary role, is paralleled in the *process* of self-discovery. Job, in his anguished individuality, alienated from his friends, cut off from everyone in the world, comes to realize that his creator is the only one he *could* be talking to—a self-discovery. So there's never a question of Job's sanity, even for the modern reader who may be alienated from a spiritual perspective of self.

The central emotion of the *Book of Job* is in the idea that man is not the center of the universe, and so he's not in a position to fully understand or judge its creator. I found my key to the poem neither in extensive textual research (though I consulted more than twenty different English translations of *Job* and a large amount of the critical literature: literary, religious, and philological) nor in my technical capacities as a poet, but in a kind of self-discovery which showed me a spiritual kinship between the expansive quality of experimental American poetry and a similar passion in the ancient Hebrew poets.

A poet like Whitman has more affinities with the Old Testament prophets than with the tradition of poetry in England. He embodies the American affection for the pragmatic while emphasizing that it is space and process which are unremittingly our condition. His feeling for individuality is predicated on an "America" as much as the prophet's concern for individuals extends a loyalty to Israel into metaphorical "Israel." In their acutely discerned orientation to God, the biblical poets resisted the esoteric and spoke to the mainstream (regardless of what it wanted to hear). There is likewise in Whitman an often radical boldness, out of his immersion in an everyday culture.

Both the Joban poet and Whitman are "gentle prophets"; their revelations come from the natural world and the speaking openness to feeling that their poetry allows. American poetry since Whitman—especially experimental poetry—has no single source for its language in the sense that it does not depend upon a poetic or literary vocabulary. Just as poets today may go beyond the classics to explore the roots of poetry itself, the Joban poet had a comparable freedom (within a disciplined ear for tradition) to incorporate spoken, liturgical, and literary language into his poem. Behind the original composer of *Job* lay not only a tradition of Wisdom literature, with its poetic practice of virtual quotation, but a popular oral tradition against which some of Job's lines no doubt echo. The *Book of Job* was written as poetry, not colloquial Hebrew, but with his ear tuned to the idiom, imagery, and phrasing of spoken language, and with a refined eye for new contexts of traditional imagery, the author created an atmosphere of spokenness. There is an inspiration from the physically *heard* reality of words, free of rhetorical gesture, in this poetry. Conversely, the practice of poetry leads back to a respect for the physical or natural world of experience.

Almost all English translations which strive for fluency lose imagery. But American poetry today has evolved a prosody from raw speech that is capable of equalling the complexity of the original Hebrew. The uncanny shifts and changes in the flow of ordinary conversation, the often surreal collage of overheard imagery, require the heightened sense of timing equal to the ear of the jazz musician-poet who composes as he performs. In an interview, just before his death, the legendary John Coltrane says, "You got to keep talking/to be real." In my own poetry I've concentrated on speech rhythms, on replaying in slow-motion the already established visionary experiment linking line and stanza to a sense of real breathing. In American poetry it's a democratic experimentation, an openness often surprising in how much it can include; its individualism is an egalitarian idiom. When I began to translate Hebrew psalms a few years ago, I was extending my practice to that mainstream which flowed to and from Whitman.

I see my role as translator to be individual, but in concept of approach rather than in display of "originality." My identity is in the approach, in the human desire to touch the original without tainting it. Ezra Pound, and particularly the poetic practice of his contemporary, Louis Zukofsky, showed me how translation could be the essence of poetry, not secondary to a poet's so-called original work—an attitude shared by the Joban poet himself in his transmission of the Job legend. Zukofsky's use of translation, whether from Latin or Hebrew, bears his originality all in *how* he presents it. "Only the eyes are individual" is his statement about the unlimited wealth of imagery in front of every person: the more carefully we're able to distinguish between images of the objective world, the more we realize that it's how we look at things that makes us unique. The uniqueness of my personality is a vehicle only, from which I step out, as from a car stopped in the desert, to walk up to the meditating poet. And so the measure of my success will be how strongly the reader of my translation is motivated to read another, if not the Hebrew text itself, because I have barely begun to realize the authenticity of its greatness; yet my approach is one of committed reverence for the original poetry.

In modern poetry the spoken voice, free of aesthetic personae, may be an agent of literal spirit, suggesting a metaphorical dialogue, a higher consciousness disembodied from the poet as he listens to *himself* speaking. In that modern tradition I came to the poem of *Job* with a sense of the veracity possible in an identification with the original author, whose passionate calling on an invisible God bursts through his Job. I struggle for a depth of literalness in my translation; for instance, just as the Joban poet drew on popular proverbial expressions for irony, I have consciously used the occasional cliché and idiom of popular culture—our "airwaves" are just as filled with contending superstition and folklore (disguised as commercials or propaganda) as were the newsbearers of the ancient Middle East. It was hardly uncommon for Hebrew poets to make ironic use of "officialese."

The poets I've learned from, like the Joban poet, are often difficult activists for new openings to conscience, consciousness raised to a self-aware response to creation. The modern tradition of experimentation with collage has freed the poet from the need to dominate his poem, to be at the center of its universe. The use of collage in poetry (such as in Apollinaire) suggests a search for visionary aesthetics in its expansion of our sense of metaphor: an infinite randomness of juxtaposition. Many contemporary biblical scholars imply a connection between biblical poetry and collage when they show that the term parallelism applies not only technically but philosophically, unfolding a visionary attitude to creativity. Like parallelism in the hands of an anonymous Hebrew poet, collage tends to disembody an authoritarian personality by its reorderings—it holds a mirror to the physical universe. In addition, American poets who explored beyond modernism, expanding it to documentary approaches (Charles Reznikoff is an example), to open-eyed meditation on language (Gertrude Stein is an example), and to self-abandoned but everyday speech (Frank O'Hara is an example), helped me feel more at home in the ancestral company of the Bible's poets.

With a historical perspective stretching back through Apollinaire's essay "The New Spirit" at the turn of the century, the tradition of experimental poetry bears in on the medium of language itself. This consciousness of linguistic context I find anchored in the poetry of the Bible, in the medium of conscience as it becomes actualized in the dialogue of man and God. The medium of biblical poetry is early Hebrew language, which is highly visual: the present tense, like the realism of a third dimension, expands out of just two tenses.

Because I wanted to recreate the intensity and visual dynamics of the original composition of *Job,* a line-by-line comparison with the Hebrew is difficult, but I do follow the original order rigorously. I wanted to be true to the flowing poetry, not just the words, of Job's speeches. Robert Gordis, in "Writing a Commentary on Job," speaks of the flow: "The two basic characteristics of biblical poetry are parallelism and, to a lesser extent, the meter patterns, which are based not on syllables, either qualitative or quantitative, but on stressed word or thought-units." And in surprisingly similar terms, here is the contemporary poet Robert Creeley characterizing Walt Whitman's poetics: "The constantly recurring structures in Whitman's writing, the insistently parallel sounds and rhythms, recall the patterns of waves as I see them daily. How can I point to *this* wave, or *that* one, and announce that it is *the* one?'' Rather than try to reconstruct the awesome museum of a literal line-by-line translation, I wanted to make the poem flow and renew itself. The *Book of Job* is not a narrative poem, but what modern poets would call a "serial" poem. Instead of a narrative climax, there's a climactic intensity that builds up in the movement of expanding repetition, deepening intensity of feeling, and the drama of Job's sheer persistence.

Here is an example of a passage with the problem of dynamic imagery diluted by weird English correspondences. Stanzas 3 through 6 of Chapter 29 read, in the King James Version:

> When his candle shined upon my head, and when by his light I walked through darkness;
>
> As I was in the days of my youth, when the secret of God was upon my tabernacle;
>
> When the Almighty was yet with me, when my children were about me;
>
> When I washed my steps with butter, and the rock poured me out riches of oil;

It does not seem hard to sense through this translation that the original imagery is too profound to be either washed over or congealed into impenetrable English. I've translated it this way:

> . . . .
> God watching over me
> the sun shining
>
> inside me
> like inner light
> ushering me past the nightmare

on the screen of giddy youth
my life was in focus
around me   it was autumn

my wife and children growing
my walks were bathed in light
in cream

the heaviest rocks in my way
smoothed out
like oil

I was as if transported
wherever I went
on a stream of affection. . .

To accept *Job* on its own terms means seeing beyond the conscious narrative or drama of its "plot" to realize its author's transcendence over his self-centered mind. The imagination behind Job's words takes us away from his (and our) nightmare into the daylight of dialogue, where we can humanize the visionary totality—conscious and unconscious—of what we can't control. Where Job fails, in his inability to transcend vanity, the Joban poet succeeds: his poem is still open to an answer, beyond *his* words, in our own struggle with language and the boundaries of self.

David Rosenberg

November, 1975
New York, New York